Welcome to
BLETCHL

GW00363931

Bletchley Park has global significance. It is where the World War Two Codebreakers decyphered seemingly impenetrable codes and cyphers, and it is where the world's first semi-programmable computers were installed and operated.

The intelligence produced here contributed to all theatres of World War Two. Bletchley Park pioneered co-operation with other intelligence services including France, Poland and the United States. The techniques developed here played a major role in the Cold War and, in many cases, remain highly relevant today.

The site is a portal into the information age in which we live, as unique data-processing machines were developed to help speed up the codebreaking effort.

Bletchley History 1938 to now

In 1938 the British Government bought part of the then much larger Bletchley Park estate, to house the most secret codebreaking and intelligence efforts of the Government Code and Cypher School (GC&CS) in a quiet rural location, easily reached from London, Cambridge and Oxford. It was fully expected that in a future war London would come under heavy air attack. Over the next few months the first wooden huts were built and communications channels were established, as war loomed.

Early in the war the Bletchley Park operation centred on the work of a small group of experts. It went on to pioneer the application of close inter-service liaison and production line methods to the key stages of the process – collection, codebreaking, evaluating and disseminating.

In late 1939 Cambridge mathematician and Codebreaker Gordon Welchman realised Enigma settings were changed at midnight every day. A 24 hour shift system was set up. The first wartime breaks into Enigma were achieved in January 1940.

From May 1940 there was a massive increase in the volume and complexity of traffic, as the theatre of war widened. The so-called Phoney War ended with the German invasion of Denmark and Norway in April 1940. A new Enigma key was introduced and it took the Codebreakers in Hut 6 six days to break it. This break into the new key told the Allies every move the German Army was making, and was about to make.

Captain Ridley's
Shooting Party 1938

By early 1943 Bletchley Park had developed from a small community of specialist cryptographers into a vast and complex global signals intelligence factory. It hit its peak in 1944, when around ten thousand people worked at Bletchley and its associated out-stations. The contributions of Bletchley Park's Codebreakers to the outcome of World War Two are now globally recognised. They include:

- Location of the U-Boat packs in the Battle of the Atlantic
- Identifying the beam guidance system for German bombers
- The Mediterranean and North African campaigns, including El Alamein
- Launch and success of Operation Overlord, including breaking German Secret Service Enigma, complementing the Double Cross operation which misled Germany on the intended target for D-Day

- Helping to identify new weapons including German V weapons, jet aircraft, atomic research and new U-Boats
- Analysis of the effect of the war on the German economy
- Breaking Japanese codes
- The outcome of the war in the Pacific

After the war, the GC&CS became Government Communications Headquarters (GCHQ) and it left Bletchley Park in 1946. The site was used as a training school for the Control Commission which governed post-war Germany, then a teacher training college, and later a training centre for the Civil Aviation Authority and the GPO, which became British Telecom. In 1992 a group of local historians saved the site from developers' bulldozers and the Bletchley Park Trust was formed to preserve the site for the nation.

The same view of The Mansion today

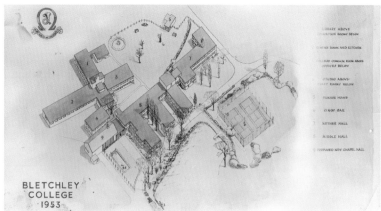

Bletchley Park in 1953

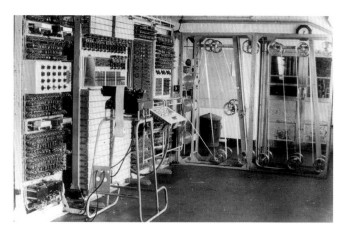

Colossus, the world's first electronic semi-programmable computer

Aerial view, 1966

Above: Bombe machine under construction

Right: Bletchley Park in 2003

Breaking Enigma

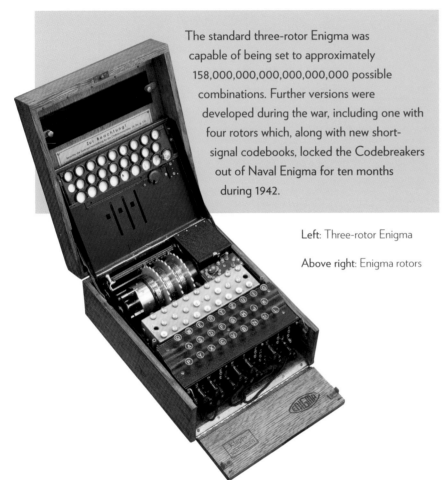

The standard three-rotor Enigma was capable of being set to approximately 158,000,000,000,000,000,000 possible combinations. Further versions were developed during the war, including one with four rotors which, along with new short-signal codebooks, locked the Codebreakers out of Naval Enigma for ten months during 1942.

Left: Three-rotor Enigma

Above right: Enigma rotors

Above: Enigma rotors with numbered ring scales (German Army or Air Force)

The Enigma used rotors to scramble messages into unintelligible cyphertext. The German military adapted an early commercial version, marketed to the banking industry, and believed it to be impenetrable. Each one of the machine's billions of possible combinations generated completely different cyphertext. Finding those settings – which were reset at midnight every day – was the challenge faced by the Codebreakers.

Before World War Two, work was being undertaken in a number of countries to break Enigma. In July 1939, aware that Poland would soon be invaded, the three Polish mathematicians who had worked on Enigma shared their work with the British and the French. By this time the Germans were changing the Enigma settings daily and the first British wartime breaks into the daily-changing Enigma code took place at Bletchley Park in January 1940.

The number of different possible settings for the Enigma machine are staggering. Each rotor could be set to any one of 26 different ring settings. Then the plug board could be set in a vast number of different ways. The settings were also different for the Army, Air Force, Navy and Secret Service, and most were changed daily. The main task of the Codebreakers was to deduce the daily Enigma settings, so the Bombe machine became vital.

Above: Bombe Room chart

Above left: Bombe drum

Above right: Rows of drums on the Bombe

The Bombe machine was developed by Alan Turing and Gordon Welchman to speed up the breaking of Enigma, so that messages were still operationally relevant. It was inspired by the 'bomba', an earlier machine designed by the Polish Cypher Bureau. The Bombe helped to deduce the day's Enigma settings, of both the rotors and the plug board, by eliminating the many incorrect possibilities.

The Codebreakers created a menu for the wiring at the back of the Bombe based on a hypothesis, known as a 'crib', of part of the original message. Cribs were often derived from regular appearances in decyphered messages of stock phrases, such as 'message number' or 'nothing significant to report'.

Above: Bombe wiring

Left: Enigma machine in use in General Heinz Guderian's command vehicle in France, May 1940

The drums on the Bombe each represented a rotor on the Enigma. The Bombe had 36 rotors, each set of three positioned one step ahead of its neighbour. The rotors were driven through all 17,576 possible positions, which took around 30 minutes.

If the hypothesis implied in the menu was tenable, the machine would stop, supplying the Codebreakers with the likely settings. The Codebreakers would then apply those settings to a modified Type X machine and type in the encyphered message. If they'd got it right, plain German text came out, in groups of five letters. All of that day's intercepted messages on that network could then be decyphered using the Type X, and the Bombe could start on the settings of another network.

The Bombe sped up the process but a great deal of deduction was required both before and after the machine was run. Breaking into the new Enigma settings was a huge intellectual feat, which the Codebreakers achieved most days, usually in the middle of the night.

Right: Part of the keyboard of a teleprinter

Below: British cypher machine, Type X

Breaking Lorenz

Even more complex than the Enigma was the Lorenz cypher machine. It was used by Hitler himself, the High Command and German Army Field Marshals. It was much bigger and heavier than the Enigma and had twelve rotors. The Codebreakers called the machine Tunny and the coded messages Fish. Cracking Lorenz, like Enigma, relied on determining the starting position of the rotors.

Lorenz used the International Teleprinter Code, in which each letter of the alphabet was represented by a series of five electrical impulses. Extra letters were generated by the rotors and added to the original text. Five of the twelve rotors followed a regular pattern and two

Above: Inside the Lorenz attachment

Left: Lorenz cypher attachment

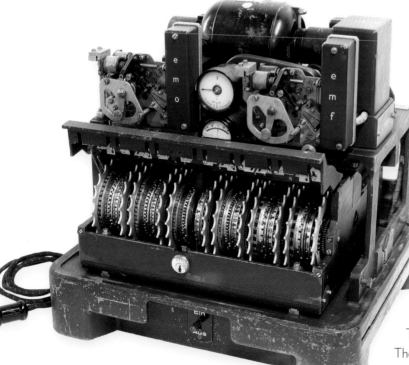

pinwheels dictated the pattern of the other five. To decrypt a message, the receiving Lorenz added the same obscuring letters.

The encyphered message was fed directly into a radio transmitter, which transmitted it to a distant receiving station. Here it was fed straight into a Lorenz machine. Both machines had to be set exactly the same way.

The Germans began using the Lorenz machine in early 1940. The Teleprinter signals were intercepted but the Codebreakers knew nothing about the machine being used to encrypt them. Then one German operator made a horrendous mistake.

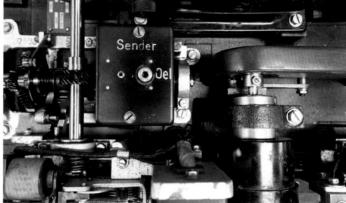

The menchanism of a Lorenz attachment

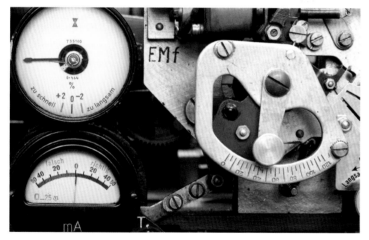

In August 1941 a long message was sent from Athens to Vienna. The operator transmitted a clear twelve-letter indicator which told the receiving operator the exact rotor start positions. He entered all 4,000 characters only to be told by the receiving operator that he hadn't got it. Assuming the system was unbreakable, the operator used the same settings and, because it was standard procedure, sent the indicator again. Therein lay his mistake. He compounded the error by using abbreviations when he re-keyed the message, because the small differences were a great help to cryptanalyst John Tiltman. It took Tiltman ten days but he recovered both German messages in full, thanks to the operator's mistake.

Bill Tutte, a Cambridge chemistry graduate, deduced through mathematical analysis how the Lorenz machine worked without ever

having seen one. A new section was set up to capitalise on Tiltman and Tutte's achievements, called The Testery after its leader Ralph Tester, a former accountant who'd lived and worked in Germany.

From mid-1942, intercepted Lorenz messages were punched into perforated Teleprinter tape and sent via both Teleprinter and dispatch rider to The Testery. There they were decyphered from gibberish to German.

By 1943 the Germans had introduced complications which made it virtually impossible to break Lorenz by hand – or brain – alone. The first machine designed by Dr Max Newman and his team in The Newmanry was christened Heath Robinson, after the cartoon designer of fantastic contraptions. It worked, but was slow and unreliable, so Max Newman called upon Tommy Flowers, a brilliant Post Office electronics engineer. Flowers designed Colossus, the world's first

Left: Colossus in operation, 1944

Above: Thyratron valves in a Colossus machine

Above right: Heath Robinson was slow and unreliable

Right: Colossus tape drive pulley

practical electronic digital and information processing machine – the forerunner of the modern computer. It used 1,500 thermionic valves (vacuum tubes) and the first Colossus machine arrived at Bletchley in December 1943.

Colossus could read paper tape at 5,000 characters per second, the paper tape in its wheels travelling at 30 miles per hour. This meant that the huge amount of mathematical work that needed to be done to break Lorenz could be carried out in hours, rather than weeks.

The first Colossus was joined by a second in June 1944, and was working in time for Eisenhower and Montgomery to be sure that Hitler had swallowed the deception plan prior to D-Day on 6 June 1944. There were eventually ten working Colossi at Bletchley Park.

Other Codes and Cyphers

Bletchley Park did not only break into Enigma and Lorenz. The Codebreakers also cracked a number of other cyphers being used by enemy forces during World War Two.

The C36 Hagelin, for example, was a Swedish commercial machine with five pinwheels. It was introduced in 1936 and France ordered five thousand. It was also used by the Italian Navy.

Above: Inside the C36 Hagelin

Left: Hagelin cypher machine

Significant effort went into breaking Japanese codes too. Around 55 different systems were used during the course of World War Two. Most were numeric but some lower-grade messages were encoded using letter-based cyphers. The sheer size of the Pacific helped the Allies, as it meant keys and codebooks were rarely replaced because it was impractical to send out new ones too often, over such great distances. So once the Allies broke into a code, they had a longer window than with other cypher systems before it was changed.

There were other cypher systems which didn't even involve machines. A book cypher codenamed Barbara is an example of paper-based codes. It was based on a double transposition system and was used by Germany to send weather reports. John Tiltman broke into this system in March 1940.

Left: Hagelin cypher wheels

Below: Relays in a Sturgeon machine

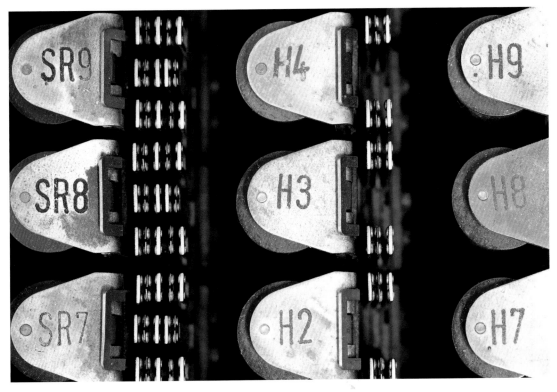

The development of the Bletchley Park site

Bletchley Park is unique. It housed a collection of brilliant minds tasked with codebreaking during World War Two, thereby altering the course of history.

The surviving fabric of Bletchley Park shows every stage of the advances made in cryptographic, computing and intelligence processes. War work at Bletchley Park began in The Mansion, then expanded into hastily built timber Huts and, later, brick, steel and concrete Blocks, most of which still stand today.

The Hut-building programme started before war even broke out. The decision to give the codebreaking operation the resources it needed to expand was given urgency by Winston Churchill himself in 1941, when he encouraged his Chiefs of Staff to 'Action this Day' requests from Bletchley. This urgency reflected the pressures of total war. The construction of the Blocks marked the Allies' transition from defensive to offensive military operations, including the bomber offensive, the break-out from North Africa and preparations for the invasion of Europe.

Above: Bletchley Park July 1940

Right: View from The Mansion in 1945

Above: View from Hut 2

Right: Map showing the development of Bletchley Park 1939-45, courtesy of English Heritage

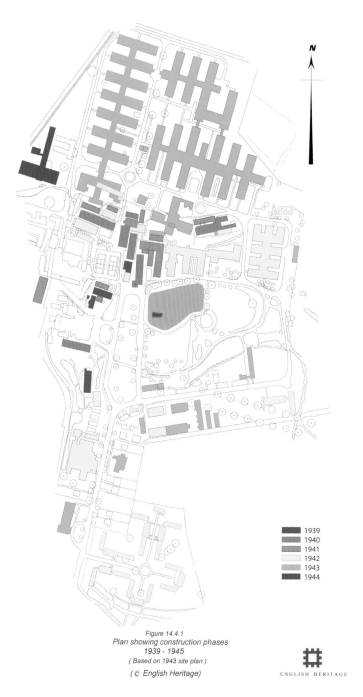

■	1939
■	1940
■	1941
□	1942
■	1943
■	1944

Figure 14.4.1
Plan showing construction phases
1939 - 1945
(Based on 1943 site plan)
(© English Heritage)

ENGLISH HERITAGE

The development of the Huts and Blocks, from the original nucleus centred on The Mansion and Stable Yard, shows how codebreaking was industrialised and is a testament to the development of information technology. Bletchley Park is now a unique surviving example of a country house and park adapted for wartime use, and typifies developments at hundreds of country homes requisitioned for use during World War Two.

The Mansion

The Mansion dates back to the late 1870s. It was bought in 1883 by Herbert Leon, a wealthy stockbroker, along with the surrounding estate and was occupied by him, his wife Lady Fanny and family. He added an opulent new south front and lavish interior around 1906.

During World War Two The Mansion served as the headquarters and recreational building. The major codebreaking sections initially worked on the ground floor, before the expansion into the Huts. The telephone exchange, Teleprinter machines and cafeteria were in the Dining Room until April 1942. The Mansion also housed the offices of senior staff such as John Tiltman, head of the Military Section, Commander Alastair Denniston, head of GC&CS from 1919 to February 1942, and Commander Edward Travis, head from 1942 and the first post-war head of GCHQ.

Denniston made clear his intention to provide facilities for relaxation from the mental stresses of work. The first meeting of the Joint Committee of Control, which ran the internal organisation of Bletchley Park from 1941 to 1942, issued a memo which read 'In my view we have reached a stage in the development of BP when our main and most serious drawback to efficiency and the sense of good feeling on which efficiency must depend, is not the absence of adequate space to work, but the absence of any place at all to play ... somewhere where all can have their cup of coffee and cigarette without condemning the vast majority, seniors and juniors alike, to stand cheek by jowl like sardines in a tin.'

Opposite left: The Mansion before World War Two

Opposite right: The Leon family's staff

Below left: The peaceful Park

Below right: Lady Fanny Leon in The Morning Room

The Mansion – known by Bletchley Park workers, both military and civilian, as The Main House – was the iconic structure of the site. The area of the Park in front of The Mansion and Stable Yard conveys the strongest sense of Bletchley Park's wartime atmosphere, and features strongly in published memoirs of wartime Bletchley.

The first telephone exchange was in the Billiard Room. Later a larger exchange was built in a blast-proof Hut immediately behind Hut 4. The building which now houses the Enigma Cinema was later built to house the main switchboard for the many Teleprinters, leaving the one behind Hut 4 for telephones. The Dining Room was used by senior members of staff only, the remainder eating in the canteen which still stands in Wilton Avenue, outside the original World War Two entrance to Bletchley Park.

Left: The Mansion

Below: Griffins guard The Mansion entrance

Left: The Mansion is architecturally diverse and unique

Above: Inside The Mansion

Codebreaker Mavis Batey (née Lever) recalls it not being quite as egalitarian as intended, though:

> 'It all sounds very jolly ... but none of the people I have spoken to remember it that way. I feel sure that the top brass didn't queue with us in the canteen but continued to use the Dining Room and other stately rooms for visiting VIPs.'

The parkland of Bletchley Park was used for playing games, drinking coffee in the open air – weather permitting – and as a place for non-smokers to clear their heads given the pipe-smoking culture which prevailed in the Huts. Entertainment and consolation were sought by the lake, which had been built more than two centuries earlier from the remains of medieval fishponds. Many romances also blossomed here.

The Mansion is open to visitors and contains information about its pre-war history.

Right: The Billiard Room

Stable Yard

During World War Two there were three cottages on the north side of the Stable Yard, the Apple and Pear Store on the south side, which later became known as The Bungalow, and the West Range, used for vehicles and carrier pigeons which received messages from occupied Europe.

Codebreakers, including Alan Turing and Dilly Knox, worked in Cottages 2 and 3 from September 1939. The first breaks into daily-changing German Enigma were made here. This success was kept secret even within Bletchley Park. The breaking of the German Secret Service (Abwehr) codes by Dilly Knox and his team, Intelligence Service Knox (ISK), in December 1941 supported the Double Cross operation prior to D-Day.

- The break into Italian Enigma that underpinned victory in the naval Battle of Matapan, off Crete in March 1941, was achieved in Cottage 3.
- Alan Turing and Gordon Welchman developed the first electromechanical Bombe in The Bungalow.

Cottage 1 was the home of the Head of Works Services, Mr Budd and his family – including twin daughters who were six years old when they arrived at Bletchley Park. The Budds were one of only two families who lived on site.

The Garages in wartime

The Garages today

Today in the Stable Yard the Polish Memorial commemorates the breathtaking achievements of the three mathematicians – Marian Rejewski, Henryk Zygalski and Jerzy Rozycki – who broke Enigma using mathematical methods in 1932, and who handed their work to the British in 1939, helping to advance the codebreaking efforts of the Allies.

Beyond the garages is the gate where most of the wartime staff and the dispatch riders arrived. As many as forty riders per hour delivered up to 3,000 messages a day.

The Stable Yard now houses the offices of the Bletchley Park Trust.

The Cottages

The Clock Tower in wartime

The Clock Tower undergoing repair

The Polish Memorial

Hut 6

Hut 6 was built in January 1940 for the decryption of Enigma messages from the German Army and Air Force, with help from the perforated sheets and then the Bombe machines in Huts 11 and 11A. The perforated sheets were also known as Zygalski sheets, after the Polish Codebreaker who invented them, and were used to help deduce the Enigma keys and wheel orders.

Once the day's Enigma settings had been partially established with help from the Bombes, the information was sent back to Hut 6 where it was used to complete the discovery of the Enigma settings. Decrypted messages were then passed to Hut 3 for translation and analysis.

A specially built chute was created to send decrypts securely to Hut 3. It was not as high-tech as many of Bletchley Park's wartime innovations; a broom handle was used to convey a wire basket containing messages between the two Huts. There were complaints about the draught coming in from the chute and a carpenter was called in to install flaps at either end. This put an end to the method of alerting the other Hut that a message was coming – calling out – and the sender moved on to banging the chute with the broom handle instead.

Hut 6 is currently derelict but will soon be restored to its wartime condition, and will open to visitors in mid-2014.

Above right: Hut 6 Control Room in Block D

Right: Machine Room, Hut 6 in Block D

Above: Inside Hut 6

Above right: Hut 6

Right: Hut 3 viewed from Hut 6

Hut 3

Once German Army and Air Force Enigma messages had been decrypted in Hut 6, they were passed next door to Hut 3 for translation and analysis. It was also the main reporting centre for encyphered Teleprinter codes, named Fish by the Codebreakers, decrypted in The Testery and Newmanry in Block F.

The translators in Hut 3 had to make German military language, strictly formatted and littered with jargon, read like a credible report from a fake spy. Most recipients were never told that a message had come from Bletchley Park, nor that it was based on intercept.

The writer and poet F.L. Lucas, who worked in Hut 3, said, 'It was not a matter of receiving straightforward messages and translating them: it was always a matter of receiving material which was nearly always more or less imperfect, often incomplete, rarely intelligible with ease, and at its worst totally meaningless to even the best German scholar.'

Hut 6 staff in Block D. Huts 3 & 6 worked as a pair.

Huts 3 & 6 are undergoing refurbishment

As the importance of the work carried out in the Huts grew, so did the number of staff needed. By 1942 Hut 3 activity was no longer housed in a single wooden structure but in a whole range of locations and buildings around the Park. This is also true of the other Huts.

Hut 3 will soon be restored to its wartime condition and will become part of the Museum in mid-2014.

Bletchley Park veteran Chris Hayes recalled, 'I was told to report to Bletchley railway station, and walk up to the main house for an interview. I was not told the nature of the work before I got there, and have kept quiet about it for the past fifty years! I was sent to Hut 3, and my younger sister Lola Horan joined me at Bletchley Park six months later and was sent to Hut 6.'

View of Hut 11 from Hut 3

The Huts were built in clusters

Hut 8

Hut 8 was built in January 1940 for the decryption of raw material from the Navy. As in Hut 6, the Codebreakers in Hut 8 used Zygalski's perforated sheets and the Bombe machine, the electromechanical device developed at Bletchley Park to speed up the elimination process in calculating the day's Enigma settings.

The first break into Naval Enigma – codenamed Dolphin – early in 1941 had a significant impact on the Battle of the Atlantic. Information decrypted in Hut 8 helped to reduce the destruction wrought by the U-Boats in the Atlantic.

Under its heads Alan Turing and then Hugh Alexander Hut 8, like Hut 6, also became a major driving force in the development of analytical machines to speed up the decryption process.

Hut 8 today

Naval Enigma was broken in Hut 8

Hut 8 at the end of the war

Hut 8 became particularly important around D-Day. By this time it had been renamed Hut 18 – to avoid confusion, rather than create it – because the Hut 8 operation had moved to one of the new brick and concrete buildings, Block D.

Alan Turing used his office in Hut 8 to write academic papers in his spare time, some of which are now on show in the Block B Turing Exhibition.

In Hut 8 visitors can see Alan Turing's office.

Above: Departments retained their Hut names when they later moved into Blocks

Right: Alan Turing chained his mug to the radiator to prevent it being stolen

Hut 4

Before the arrival of GC&CS, the Library in The Mansion looked out over a beautiful rose garden. Hut 4 had been built over the latter by August 1939.

By early 1940 this was used for translating and analysing German Naval Enigma messages decrypted by Hut 8. These two Huts provided crucial day-to-day intelligence in the desperate battles between the Allied convoys and the U-Boats which were determined to cut Britain's vitally important supply lines across the Atlantic.

Hut 4 viewed through The Mansion windows

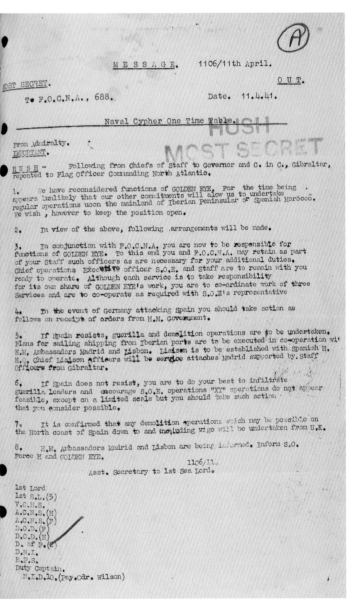

'Most Secret' later became 'Top Secret'

Hut 4 also played a key role in the D-Day landings. The Double Cross deception, codenamed Operation Fortitude South, led the Germans to believe that the Allied plan to invade Normandy was actually a diversion from the true target, the Pas de Calais. This allowed the Allies to land at Normandy while the Germans laid in fortified wait in Calais. Messages processed in Hut 4 made it clear that Germany had swallowed the deception whole.

Early in the war, relations between the Naval Section in Hut 4 and the Admiralty were strained, as many in Naval Intelligence were unconvinced of the reliability of information emerging from Bletchley Park. But in 1941 the Enigma being used by the U-Boats, codenamed Dolphin, was broken thanks to a combination of repetitive weather transmissions and a captured book of Enigma keys. This was a major breakthrough. Dolphin was broken and then read every day until the end of the war.

Today Hut 4 houses the café.

Above right: Hut 4 was built in close proximity to the Codebreakers' offices in The Mansion

Right: Hut 4 houses the café

Huts 11 & 11A

Hut 11 was built to house the Bombe machines developed by Alan Turing and Gordon Welchman to speed up the daily search for the Enigma cypher keys used by the German Army, Air Force, Navy and Secret Service. It replaced a smaller, wooden Hut, the concrete structure providing the protection needed for such precious machines.

Bombes were mass produced. Two whole buildings at Bletchley Park were given over to housing them, and there were far more at out-stations in local villages and as far away as Eastcote and Stanmore on the outskirts of London. Even more were produced and operated in the United States. Hut 11A became the main control centre for all Bombes in the UK.

Hut 11A was built in March 1942, as more Bombes were needed and made, and it also became a training centre for the Women's Royal Navy Service – WRNS, nicknamed 'Wrens' – who operated the machines and recall the Hut being hot and noisy.

Wrens operated the Bombe machines

Huts 11 & 11A, the Bombe Huts

The first Newmanry was established here in 1943, under Max Newman. This section developed machines to help decypher German teleprinter codes. These two Huts provided a highly secure environment for the crucial machines.

Hut 11A is currently being restored and is due to open in autumn 2013. Hut 11 is open to the public.

Bombe machines in Hut 11A

Hut 11 dressed for ITV drama The Bletchley Circle

Hut 1

Hut 1 was one of the first Huts to be built. Its first purpose was to house the MI6 wireless transmission station which was originally in The Mansion's water tower. Aerials were strung from The Mansion to the tall trees at the front.

The first Bombe machine, Victory, was tested in Hut 1 in 1940, in what was then a sick bay. Later in the war Hut 1 became the Transport Office. A mere handful of the Codebreakers lived on site, the rest being billeted around Bletchley and the surrounding countryside and having to get to and from the site in large numbers for the three eight-hour shifts each day and night.

Hut 1 housed the radio transmission station originally installed in The Mansion's water tower

Radio equipment in Hut 1

Hut 12

Hut 12 started as an annexe to Hut 3, and later became part of Hut 4's Naval Enigma operation. It then housed the Intelligence Exchange, with cryptanalyst Nigel de Grey at the helm.

Ian Fleming, the James Bond creator, worked for MI6 and was responsible for liaising with Bletchley Park. He planned an operation, Operation Ruthless, which never came to fruition, but the qualities he described in the operative it would need were remarkably similar to the 007 character he later created.

By April 1943 Hut 12 was known as the Education Hut, used for chamber music classes and orchestral evenings held by the BP Musical Society.

Today Hut 12 is open to the public.

Above: Hut 12

BP Musical Society used Hut 12

A
CONCERT OF
ENGLISH MUSIC
BY THE
B.P. MUSICAL SOCIETY
(Conductor - HERBERT MURRILL)
IN THE
Assembly Hall, Wilton Avenue,
FRIDAY, SEPT. 8th,
SATURDAY, SEPT. 9th,
MONDAY, SEPT. 11th,
TUESDAY, SEPT. 12th,
at 8 p.m. sharp.

Programme : Sixpence.

All Proceeds to
The Sailors', Soldiers' and Airmens' Families Association.

Creativity thrived at Bletchley Park

Block A

In May 1941 a decision was made which would alter the landscape and layout of Bletchley Park forever. The codebreaking factory had outgrown The Mansion, Cottages and wooden Huts and a programme of building more permanent brick and concrete Blocks was begun.

The first of these was Block A. There was still a significant threat of air attack so Blocks A and B, which were built at the same time, were bomb-proofed and shrouded by trees, more being planted to break up shadows thrown by the moon.

Blocks A and B were meant to house all three sections, Naval, Air and Army, but by mid-1943 the Naval Section had taken over Block A, such was the volume of messages they were decoding. Huge charts of the Atlantic covered the walls.

Today much of Block A is commercial offices.

Above: Steel, brick and concrete Blocks were built from 1941

Left: Some Blocks were reinforced against bomb blasts

Block E

Block E was the hub of outward communication from Bletchley Park. Messages were re-encyphered using Type X machines and transmitted to Allied headquarters.

Special Communication Units (SCUs) passed the highly sensitive Ultra intelligence to a Special Liaison Unit (SLU). An SLU officer would personally deliver the Ultra message to the Allied commander in the field, allow him to read and absorb, then destroy it.

No mention was made of Bletchley Park. Cover stories were used, such as 'a reliable source recovered a flimsy of a message in the wastepaper basket of ...'. To avoid enemy suspicion that Enigma was being read, information had always to be verified, and reconnaissance aircraft were sometimes sent, merely so they might be spotted by the enemy.

Block E is currently used as commercial office space.

Charts covered the walls for calculations and mapping

Block E was a communications hub

Secrecy was absolute

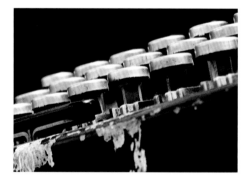

Type X machines were used to re-encrypt outgoing messages

Block B

Block B was built along with Block A, as Bletchley Park grew into a mechanised codebreaking factory. Block B was hardened, like Block A, in case of attack.

In mid-1942 the Naval Enigma Section moved here from Hut 4.

The German Navy had introduced a fourth rotor to the Enigma machines being used by the U-Boats. This vastly increased the number of possible settings. Shaun Wylie, head of the Hut 8 Crib Section, said, 'We knew it was coming. But it was a grim time. We realised that our work meant lives and it ceased to be fun.'

Block B included a section known as The Testery, led by Ralph Tester, set up to break into the Lorenz cypher system used by Hitler and his high command. This section later expanded into Block F.

Today Block B houses the main exhibitions of the Bletchley Park Museum.

Block B houses the largest collection of Enigma machines on public display anywhere in the world

Buildings were stripped out and re-allocated as the operation expanded and was re-organised

Slate statue of Alan Turing by Stephen Kettle

Blocks F & H

All that remains of Block F today is a concrete step and a patch of grass. But during World War Two it was the world's first purpose-built computer centre.

The Newmanry and The Testery moved in with Colossus, the world's first working semi-programmable computer, invented by engineer Tommy Flowers to speed up the breaking of the fiendishly complex Lorenz cypher.

> The first Colossus arrived at Bletchley Park in 1943. By the end of the war there were ten. Donald Michie, a member of The Newmanry, said, 'Each one was like a very big wardrobe. It was a scene you didn't see again until about 1960 with huge main-frames, going flat out around the clock.'

Lorenz (aka Tunny) Room

Block F also housed the Japanese codebreaking sections. It was demolished in 1988.

Block H was built in 1944 and housed Colossus and Robinson machines.

Today Block H houses The National Museum of Computing.

The Testery was housed in Block F

Block C

Names of people, places, cover names, military units, radio stations and many other significant details were recorded and kept in an enormous index, punched onto cards using Hollerith machines. Clerks, mainly women, searched decyphered messages for details that might help the Codebreakers in the future, and built up a huge cross-referencing system. At its peak, two million cards per week were used.

This was originally housed in Hut 7 under the leadership of Frederic Freeborn, but in November 1942 it moved to the new, soundproofed, brick-built Block C. Different machines were used for punching the cards, sorting and collating, and they varied in size from similar to a typewriter up to a piano. Although it was a tried and tested technology, the machines were continually adapted in conditions of absolute secrecy.

Block C is currently undergoing renovation and will open as the new visitor centre in mid-2014.

Card Index files in Block C

Block C, the home of the Card Index

Machine Room, Block C

Block C before refurbishment began

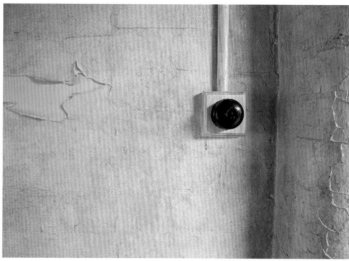

Despite post-war use, many original wartime features remain

The level of secrecy the Codebreakers worked under is difficult to imagine in the information age we live in today. Bletchley Park provided the Allies with an unprecedented wealth of intelligence on the enemy's movements and plans. Churchill gave this information the codename Ultra. Only a handful of top commanders were privileged to receive it, but were forbidden to act upon it until the Germans had been deceived into thinking the information could have come from another source. The need-to-know principle was paramount, even at Bletchley Park itself. Few staff knew the whole story or even which other sections existed besides their own, much less what they all did.

Block C became derelict after falling out of use in the late 1980s

Block D

Block D was built for secrecy, both inside and out. Its layout – with spurs off a corridor – was designed to keep different departments separate, so that staff knew only what they needed to. Around a thousand people worked here and a pneumatic tube system and conveyor belt were installed to speed up communication.

One spur housed the American contingent. The number of United States personnel connected to Bletchley Park eventually reached around three hundred. It was here that the 'special relationship', initiated politically by Winston Churchill and President Roosevelt, was firmly cemented into British-United States affairs.

Several sections moved here when they outgrew the Huts, including Naval, Army and Air Force Enigma, the reporting centre for encyphered Teleprinter traffic from The Testery and Newmanry, and the Intelligence Exchange. Much intelligence planning and decoding for the Normandy invasion took place within these walls.

Sovex convey system in Block D

Block D remains derelict

One key figure in the D-Day deception, which led Hitler to believe the Normandy landings were a diversionary tactic to draw his troops away from the real target, the Pas de Calais, was a Spanish spy named Garbo. He was a double agent, who invented a network of no less than 27 fictitious spies, claiming expenses for them all from Germany. Bletchley Park was able to read messages sent between the German Secret Service (Abwehr) and Garbo's controller in Spain, which showed that the Abwehr fully believed the deception.

Block D also gives us an idea of how the now demolished Block F might have looked.

Block D is currently derelict and the Bletchley Park Trust has long-term plans to restore and open it to the public.

US serviceman working at Bletchley Park

An imposing entrance to Block D

People

During World War One Britain built up a significant Signals Intelligence operation, listening to enemy radio traffic. The Government Code & Cypher School (GC&CS) was created at the end of the war and developed over the next two decades. By 1939 veteran cryptanalysts from World War One plus linguists and classicists such as John Tiltman, Dilly Knox, Hugh Foss and Frank Birch formed the core of GC&CS's expertise. They were joined by men and women recruited from industry and other branches of academia. This eclectic mix of people, together with the rarefied atmosphere of Bletchley Park and the great sense of its work's importance, made for a unique experience.

The Bletchley Park Recreational Club included a library, drama group, music and choral societies as well as bridge, chess, fencing and Scottish dancing. Wrens drafted in to operate the Bombes were billeted together at local country houses including Woburn Abbey, and the Wrenneries became renowned for their dances.

Rounders on the Lawn

Bletchley Park had a thriving amateur dramatics scene

Skating on the Lake, January 1940

Musical and theatrical productions were popular

Fencing at BP

Many romances blossomed here, and numerous couples went on to marry. But they had all signed the Official Secrets Act and kept their vow of silence until the story of what was achieved here began to emerge in the 1970s. Then, and even now, some remain tight-lipped about their part in the codebreaking operation because they had sworn to do so.

Many of the Codebreakers went on to achieve high positions in academia, business and politics after the war. Some played a key role in developing GCHQ, as GC&CS was renamed.

Women made up the majority of the personnel at Bletchley Park, and not only in supporting roles: they made a significant contribution to the codebreaking. The working culture was described by American cryptographer William Friedman as one where 'Rank or status cuts no ice.'

Women outnumbered men at Bletchley Park by around three to one

Restoration

Bletchley Park was the Home of the Codebreakers during World War Two and is where the modern computer age began, heralding the digital era we live in now.

Today many of the wartime Huts, which were erected in haste at a time of urgent operational need and designed to last only a few years, are still standing – more by an accident of history than design.

Until 1974 the work of the Codebreakers at Bletchley Park was Britain's best-kept secret. The first book about the wartime achievements here was written by Frederick Winterbotham, and it sent ripples of shock through the veterans' community. Ever since, interest in what happened here has grown. In 1992 the Bletchley Park Trust was formed to preserve the historic buildings for the nation. It has saved the site from the bulldozers a number of times, and managed – often against the odds – to develop the museum you see today as well as a thriving educational programme.

Today the project to restore Bletchley Park is expected to cost in the order of £20 million and take ten years to complete. The Trust aims to enable the site to receive up to 250,000 visitors a year, generate new displays aimed at a wider audience and restore the site closer to its World War Two atmosphere.

The Trust has completed fundraising for the first phase of the project, costing £7.4 million. Fundraising is now under way for the second phase, which aims to expand further the site, educational programme and exhibitions.

> 'The work here at Bletchley Park ... was utterly fundamental to the survival of Britain and to the triumph of the West. I'm not actually sure that I can think of very many other places where I could say something as unequivocal as that. This is sacred ground. If this isn't worth preserving, what is?'
>
> Professor Richard Holmes, Military Historian

Roof repairs

Hut 3 today

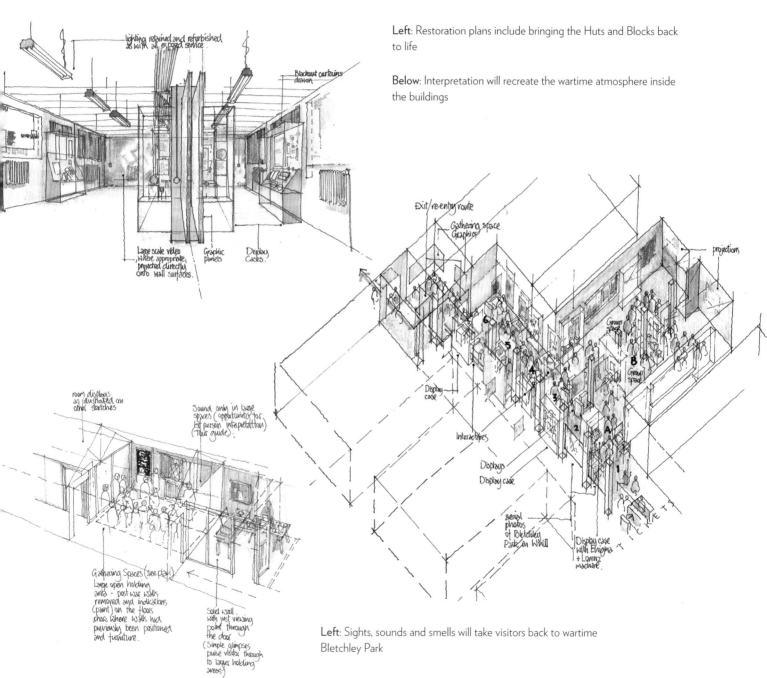

lighting retained and refurbished with all exposed service

Blackout curtains drawn

Large scale video where appropriate projected directly onto wall surfaces.

Graphic panels

Display Cases.

Left: Restoration plans include bringing the Huts and Blocks back to life

Below: Interpretation will recreate the wartime atmosphere inside the buildings

Exit/re-entry route

Gathering space Graphics

projections

Group space

Group space

Display case

Interactives

Displays

Display case

aerial photos of Bletchley Park in WWII

Display case with Enigma + Lorenz machine.

TICKETS

room displays as illustrated on other sketches

Sound only in large spaces (opportunity for 1st person interpretation) (Tour guide).

Gathering Spaces (see plan). Large open holding area - post war walls removed and indications (paint) on the floors shows where walls had previously been positioned and furniture.

Solid wall with just viewing point through the door (Simple glimpses pulse visitor through to larger holding areas)

Left: Sights, sounds and smells will take visitors back to wartime Bletchley Park

The Impact of Bletchley Park

Winston Churchill, the British Prime Minister, was an ardent supporter of Bletchley Park and had absolute belief in the intelligence generated by the Codebreakers, referring to them as 'the geese that laid the golden egg and never cackled'. When the top Codebreakers wrote to him in 1941, starved of resources to do their essential work, Churchill ordered 'Action this day! Make sure they have all they want on extreme priority and report to me that this has been done.'

'The intelligence ... from you [Bletchley Park] ... has been of priceless value. It has saved thousands of British and American lives and, in no small way, contributed to the speed with which the enemy was routed and eventually forced to surrender... [It was a] very decisive contribution to the Allied war effort.'

General Dwight D. Eisenhower

'Ultra shortened the war by not less than two years and probably by four years; moreover, in the absence of Ultra, it is uncertain how the war would have ended.'

Sir Harry Hinsley, official historian of British Intelligence in World War Two

Public Memorial for Veterans of Bletchley Park and its Outstations dedicated by HM The Queen in 2011